Animating the Golden Rule... An Introduction
Teachers Guidebook

Revised Date: 17/08/2014
Soft Cover ISBN # 978-0-9868385-0-7

To order additional copies of this guide contact:

Visionary Media Inc.
283 Danforth Av. Suite 188
Toronto Ontario, Canada M4K 1N2

Cover Layout and Inside Design by A. Connolly
Photographs and Artwork copyright Scarboro Missions

Visionary Media Inc.
All rights reserved
www.thegoldenrulemovie.com
©2014

Animating the Golden Rule

An Educators Guidebook

www.thegoldenrulemovie.com

The Golden Rule and the Global Human Family

"We should act toward other nations as we wish them to act toward us."
- Millard Fillmore (1800-1874), 13th President of the United States

The Golden Rule (also known as the Ethic of Reciprocity) is arguably the most consistent, prevalent and universal ethical principle in history. It is found worldwide throughout cultures, religions, secular philosophies and indigenous traditions. Many people regard it as the most concise and general principle of ethics.

Gold itself has symbolic value and a psychological appeal that spans cultures throughout history. As a metaphor, it points to what is most pure, noble, enduring and ideal in human experience. Gold was long considered the most valuable of metals throughout the world. It is therefore no surprise that the Golden Rule contains a "gold" metaphor since, as a principle, it is prized in almost all societies.

The principle of the Golden Rule has been valued by human societies for thousands of years. Why does it deserve renewed attention today? And what special significance does the Golden Rule have for this generation of young people?

The Golden Rule is often thought of as a rule for individuals: a person must consider how he or she would wish to be treated when deciding how to treat others. However, our changing world invites us to broaden this rule to groups of people and society as a whole.

Many regions of the world, including our own country, are quickly becoming more multicultural, with people of many cultures and religions working to find ways to live together in harmony. The Golden Rule, with roots in a wide range of the world's religions and cultures, is well-suited to be the standard to which different cultures can appeal in resolving conflicts. As the world becomes more of a single interacting global community, the need for such a common standard is becoming more urgent. The Golden Rule can be the ethical cornerstone as the human family works together to build a peaceful, just and sustainable global society.

Because the Golden Rule is a point of agreement and a common denominator among so many of the world's cultures, races, and religions, it has tremendous capacity for promoting social justice, non-violence, unity, the teaching of compassion and ethics, multicultural and multifaith cooperation and more.

Today we are living in a global village. Accordingly, we are all global citizens in addition to belonging to our particular groups, races, cultures, religions and nations. Being a global citizen brings both privileges and responsibilities. The Golden Rule may be the best guide we have for bringing all the world's people to live together in peace.

Paul McKenna / Scarboro Missions
Creator of the Golden Rule poster

Table of Contents

Page

The Golden Rule Across the World's Religions Thirteen Sacred Texts

Bahá'í Faith Lay not on any soul a load that you would not wish to be laid upon you, and desire not for anyone the things you would not desire for yourself. *Bahá'u'lláh*, **Gleanings**	
Buddhism Treat not others in ways that you yourself would find hurtful. *The Buddha*, **Udana-Varga 5.18**	
Christianity In everything, do to others as you would have them do to you; for this is the law and the prophets. *Jesus*, **Matthew 7:12**	
Confucianism One word which sums up the basis of all good conduct….loving-kindness. Do not do to others what you do not want done to yourself. *Confucius*, **Analects 15.23**	
Hinduism This is the sum of duty: do not do to others what would cause pain if done to you. **Mahabharata 5:1517**	
Islam Not one of you truly believes until you wish for others what you wish for yourself. *The Prophet Muhammad*, **Hadith**	

Jainism One should treat all creatures in the world as one would like to be treated. *Mahavira*, **Sutrakritanga 1.11.33**	
Judaism What is hateful to you, do not do to your neighbour. This is the whole Torah; all the rest is commentary. Go and learn it. *Hillel, Talmud, Shabbath 31a*	
Native Spirituality We are as much alive as we keep the earth alive. *Chief Dan George*	
Sikhism I am a stranger to no one; and no one is a stranger to me. Indeed, I am a friend to all. **Guru Granth Sahib, p.1299**	
Taoism Regard your neighbour's gain as your own gain and your neighbour's loss as your own loss. *Lao Tzu*, **T'ai Shang Kan Ying P'ien, 213-218**	
Unitarianism We affirm and promote respect for the interdependent web of all existence of which we are a part. **Unitarian principle**	
Zoroastrianism Do not do unto others whatever is injurious to yourself. **Shayast-na-Shayast 13.29**	

Prepared by Paul McKenna / © Scarboro Missions, 2009

How to use this DVD to create a
Golden Rule Retreat / Workshop

Dear Educators, Youth Workers, Pastors and other users of this DVD Program:

The workshop/ retreat model referenced in this Guidebook is the result of some 20 years of research, trial and error, teacher and youth feedback. In my capacity as Retreat Director and Youth Educator, I have come to develop a process aimed at holistic (embodied) learning and transformation. Through the use of games, music, media, interactive activities, presentations, drama, art, meditation and hospitality - we seek to break down barriers that separate us from our deeper selves and from others. In the process of seeing and experiencing "*Oneness*" our ultimate hope is to put youth in touch with an evolving global consciousness of "*One Human Family*."

The DVD Program *"Animating the Golden Rule - An Introduction..."* gives both educators and students alike a helpful background to the STRENGTHS of the Golden Rule as a tool for Peace and Social Justice. The DVD is intended to inspire adult teachers and leaders of youth to create and lead Golden Rule Workshops. Furthermore, the DVD can be screened to young people prior to the workshop or at the beginning of a retreat day as a stimulus to spark their own motivation to enter into processes like the youth in the film. This Guidebook contains a more detailed overview of what is portrayed in the film and offers an approach and process that can be geared to create workshop days for youth on: Social Justice Issues, World Religions, Ethics and Values, Cultural Diversity, Ecological and Environmental Issues etc.

Whatever the workshop, this interactive process encourages participants to drop artificially imposed barriers to learning, and invites them to gradually experience what is best termed *"embodied learning."* In addition to exercising their analytical minds, this process encourages young people to access intuitive right brain learning through interactive presentations, games, movement, art, drama, meditation and media resources. Our goal is not to fill overloaded minds with more information but to create an environment and experience where transformative learning can take place.

Kathy Murtha / Director
Mission Centre Toronto, 2014

Developing Your Own Golden Rule Retreat

Getting Started:

You have everything you need around you to develop a meaningful Golden Rule Workshop for your community.

The greatest resource you have is yourself, your life story and gifts.
- Where have you experienced the Golden Rule, or the lack of it in your own life?
- What have been your own struggles and triumphs in practicing the tenets of the Golden Rule?
- What stories of hope have you experienced yourself or witnessed?

Over the past 2 decades, we have learned that you cannot engage young people unless you open up the treasure house of your own life experience. Without personal authenticity and integration young people tune out. Young people today demand authenticity, and if that is lacking and standard modules used without real life experience framework, we have found that they tune out learning. We have discovered that the best successes come from designing the day in such a way as to highlight and make use of your own talents and those of your team members. These might be: acting, storytelling, dancing , music etc... The more you give expression to your own story and gifts, the more young people will be willing to risk bringing their own lives and talents to the day. You will discover for yourselves - that if you take risks it becomes contagious!

After tapping into your own resources, it's time to look with fresh eyes at the bigger community around you.
- What possible resources are there in your own midst?
- Look around especially for artists with global sensitivities and people of various cultures and religious traditions who are deeply rooted and inspired by their background and have their own Golden Rule stories.

Examples of Resource People who spurred new variations on Golden Rule Workshops:

Ryan - a Grade 11 student approached us looking for a Co-op job placement. He had a great interest in World Religions. After witnessing what we were doing, he took the initiative to put together an excellent teaching tool in the form of an interactive flash of the Golden Rule poster, complete with symbols, music and rich historical background.

Cathy - a music composer, worked with our youth to compose their own Golden Rule Song. A week after the workshop she presented students with a copy of their very own CD, which was then used at various school events throughout the year.

David - an actor , developed a one-man presentation on the Underground Railway which led to enlivened discussions on human trafficking and slavery.

Durkhani - an Afghani refugee escaped by foot through treacherous mountains to Pakistan with her mother and little sister in hand - while her brother and father (both physicians) were being imprisoned and tortured. She was able to share Muslim embodied prayer with the youth and inspire them with her own personal story of courage and compassion.

Tina Petrova's award winning film "Rumi: Turning Ecstatic" introduced students to Rumi, the 13th. Century Sufi mystic from the Middle East, whose life and poetry transcended the narrow boundaries that separated the people of his time. Rumi lived and taught in the same region as St. Francis of Assisi and they shared similar world views; with the formalization of Tonglen Meditation (Buddhist) in the far east, these various elements formed a special Golden Rule Workshop on "Global Channels of Peace."

Terry - a local drumming instructor, brought a few dozen drums. She led students in various rythyms (ie. call and response) and shared the history and spiritual meaning of drums on several continents.

Overview of the Program

Welcome/Hospitality
It is important to create a safe, warm space where young people are welcomed with hot beverages and snacks. We have found that many high school youth skip breakfast, if left to their own devices! That makes for a downward spiral in energy and lack of motivation. In the spirit of the Golden Rule extending hospitality from the start, rather than presenting them with an imposed agenda or information, instills within them a sense of their own importance.

Introduction to the Day, Theme and Facilitators
We display the Golden Rule Poster prominently at the front of the room and impart the background of the Golden Rule as a universal tool for peace.

Resources:
Ryan Nutter's Golden Rule Interactive Flash (free download) is available from **www.scarboromissions.ca**

NOTE: Navigate to the itemized bar at the far left, click on Golden Rule and open the circle titled Golden Rule Interactive Flash.

Input:
Key presentations of the day should be engaging, interactive and contain humor. It is best not to go longer than 45-50 minutes. We we have found that invited guests willing to share stories, symbols and activities really captivate youth and engage them wholeheartedly.

Games/Humorous Exercises
Through specially chosen games and exercises, we break down young people's resistance to sharing and encourage them to demonstrate their gifts & talents.

Young People's Embodiment of the Golden Rule
Having opened up the students to some extent to a degree of playfulness - they are now encouraged to embody - one or several - versions of the Golden Rule through drama, chant, cheer, tableau, art, music, movement etc...

LUNCH

Second Input or Follow Up Activities
This is a 2nd, shorter interactive presentation or activity that follows up from the morning. You could explore a particular issue in our world today where the Golden Rule can be applied. You could organize a drumming circle where participants can experience the power and joy of working together to create harmony. You could take a nature hike and discuss, as our native people have always known - that the Golden Rule applies to Mother Earth and all her creatures.

Reflection
This is an extremely critical part of the process. Some form of quiet reflection and silence allows the young people to integrate the learning's of the day and opens them up to the possibility of personal transformation and planetary action.

Send Off Song
It's important to end the day on an upbeat note. Locate a good send off song/ CD/ Music Video - that will give the young people a sense of hope and send them off as ambassadors of the Golden Rule!

Appendix A   ICE - BREAKERS

Suggested Time Allotted: 10 - 20 mins. to disarm youth and to loosen them up

Materials: students and their hands

Gather Participants in a circle.
- Discuss the circle as a symbol of shared leadership
- Notice how each participant has equal value in a circle - no leaders, rulers etc.

Welcome to the Golden Rule Retreat
Have retreatants lace fingers and look to see which thumb is on top
- Ask if one way is better than the other?
- Why do some favour right over left?
- Why do we fall into comfortable patterns?
- Where do we see this in terms of opinions and ways of thinking in the world?
- Can we see patterns of seeing in our life?

Have participants lace fingers the other way
- Ask how it feels? Weird? Strange? Uncomfortable? Not Natural?
- Might trying to see from another's perspective be like that?
- Can we be open to "stretching" ourselves and our perspectives today on this retreat?
- Can we try on attitudes that might feel strange at first?

Open Hands Reflection
- Ask students to ball up their fists into a tight clench
- How does this feel?
- Can we sustain this tight closed-ness for long?
- Can we see how we live like this in certain ways each day?

Request … Now slowly unfurl your fingers and feel the flood of relief and relaxation as you let go … and listen to the words of a reflection about being open to the day

Introduce the Golden Rule
- Who knows what the Golden Rule is? Who said it? Have you heard it anywhere else?
- Look at the poster … there is a golden rule for all faith traditions of the globe. In fact, all peoples who have made community on the Earth have mentioned some version of the Golden Rule: *Treat others, as You Yourself would want to be treated*
- Read various Golden Rules and reflect on various faith traditions' symbols - or use the interactive flash presentation to guess the origins of spiritual music and the faith tradition
- Look at various peace-builders through history - Gandhi, Mother Teresa, Jean Vanier, Oscar Romero, Aung San Suu Kyi, Rumi and examine how their lives and actions reflected the Golden Rule

NOTES for Retreat Leaders:
Collect inspirational quotes from speeches, poems, reflections and essays that show modern shared leadership and shared leadership *"circle power,"* as opposed to single leader *"pyramid power"*.

Appendix B   GOLDEN RULE INTERACTIVE FLASH / FAITH SYMBOLS

Suggested Time Allotted: 15 to 45 minutes, depending on how in-depth the group wants to interactively look at faith symbols and commonalities around the world

Materials:

- The Golden Rule Interactive Flash -
  www.scarboromissions.ca
  NOTE: navigate to The Golden Rule section of the website, for an extensive list of free educator downloads.
- Costumes, props
- Bible, Koran, Upanishads, Torah etc.
- Religious symbols and artifacts
- Musical cds
- Instruments: gong, bells, drums, tambourines, shakers

Golden Rule Interactive Flash

Allow youth to choose a religion/culture and listen to the associated music. Have them look at the main symbol and use the prepared interactive prayers, songs, chants, symbols, texts, costumes etc to let them learn from and embody. This is the key part of the institute's introduction and will be expanded upon in preparatory workshops for teachers and retreat facilitators.

Optional: Guest Speakers from various cultures and faiths.

Additional Suggestions: Consider beginning to build a trunk of faith-related costumes, symbols, props, artifacts, stories and music for these workshops

NOTE: Your group can focus on as few as one faith tradition and build the exercises around that - or all the way up to the 13 featured on the poster.

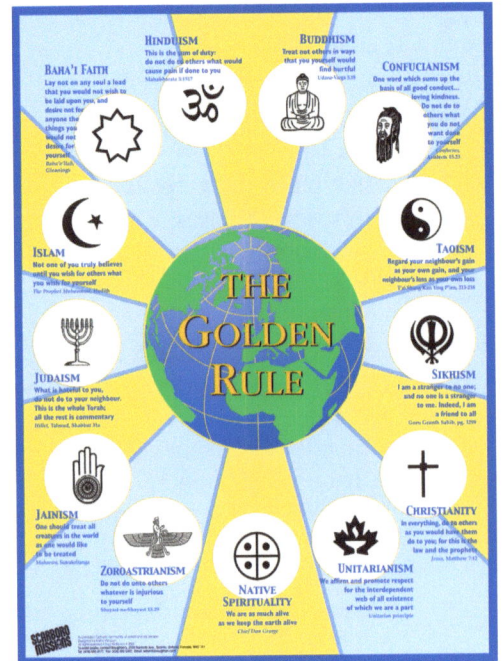

Appendix C SCAVENGER HUNT

Suggested Time Allotted: 30 mins. +15 mins. preparation time for presentations
This scavenger hunt is essential to the process of opening participants for the sharing and appreciating of each other's gifts and prepares them for the culminating exercise of the Golden Rule skits.

Materials: employ what students have on them, around them and what they can do as a team.

Sample ideas: Show us
- a spiritual artifact - cross or yin-yang symbol etc
- a picture of a family member - cell phone pics allowed
- best animal impersonation (solo or in pairs)
- longest hoola - hooper
- most original special talent - splits, double jointed, can make music with sounds

Optional Materials: costumes, fabric, hats, lipsticks, symbols

Game Format:
- Divide retreatants equally into three or more groups and let them decide a team name relating to the golden rule. For example - Team Unity, The Equalizers, The Global Village People, or the Native Dream Catchers, the Singing Seikhs, Courageous Christians etc.
- Discuss from the outset that there will be points, but that if there are winners, then that creates losers, which is not in the spirit of the Golden Rule … once we tally points at the end of the game, we will discuss the game's outcome
- Each team sends a member up the center to bring forth the scavenger hunt item requested … first there gets 20 point, second gets ten
- The game builds in momentum (natural competition) as the groups become more united and at ease …

Pose the question on the chalkboard or flip chart:
Discuss how we determine the "best" in the spirit of the Golden Rule?
- A secret ballot?
- A positive attribute for each…. ie - best sound effect, best use of prop, best group unity etc …
- Reflect on how our competitive world of winners and losers can be in direct opposition to the concept of to do unto others what we would do to ourselves.

Final Culmination of the Scavenger Hunt (as follows in Appendix D)
The final request of each group is to come up with a skit, scene, song, rap, dance, choral poem etc that depicts "The Golden Rule".
- A group could choose to embody the golden rule of a particular religion and find a creative way to present it.
- Where in our lives do we see the Golden Rule NOT being applied?
- How can we change this?
- Where are there signs of hope?
- How would it look if we DID live by the Golden Rule?
- How can we celebrate this common denominator in all faiths?

NOTES for Retreat Leaders:
Use every opportunity when competitiveness occurs to stop the game and ask the students if there is a way to consider another team's loss as our loss/another team's gain as our gain … leave space for valuable discussion of this.

Appendix D DRAMA SKITS

Suggested Time Allotted: 30 mins. + 10 mins. sharing

Materials:
- Fabric / costumes
- Prayer beads
- hats
- religious symbols
- musical instruments

Format of Dramatic presentation:

The ice breakers and the scavenger hunt at the top of the day will have encouraged a sense of *"exploration"* and offered up *"hidden skills and talents"*. It is these special skills and talents that will reveal to the groups formed - who has leadership abilities, vocal gifts, gymnastic gifts etc.

NOTE: For the previous Scavenger Hunt exercise - we asked for 4 – 5 outgoing young men or women to head up teams; they got to choose a right hand girl or boy to lead their team to victory! We then asked the remaining students to pick a winning team they want to join, and we try to ensure that each group has an equal mix of male and female (excepting private girls and boys schools).

Hand out a one sheet of the Golden Rules and ask the teams to choose a golden rule they think they have the talents and gifts within their group to animate in a unique way.

We then offer the groups various spaces to rehearse and make noise etc. It is good to have a multi- room option for rehearsal purposes. If this is not possible, we try to give them adequate space apart to create in a large gym, or some can work outside in good weather.

Give each group 20-30 minutes to work together on a scene, skit, song, etc...on the theme *"How we see the Golden Rule applied (or not applied) in our daily lives"*. Outcomes are limitless!

Facilitators oversee how participants co-operate, generate ideas, share the leadership and distribute responsibilities and recognize varied gifts … discuss with groups as they prepare their skits together - offer props, music, pens and paper.

A fun variance from the skit exercise, is to have the teams create a *"team cheer"* which employs the team name.
For example - *"We are the Native dream catchers ...... C A T C H E R S .....and we catch bad attitude and turn it into good Native — Dreamcatchers!"* Employing cheerleading moves, jumps, splits etc.

Pose the question on the chalkboard or flip chart:
Presentation of skit, scenes, songs, etc..
- Reflect on, as an actor how would I like to be treated by the audience?
- Can we, as audience be respectful spectators in the spirit of the Golden Rule?
- Watch all presentations and then discuss how we will award merit … secret vote? Best attribute? (best song, best rap, best group effort, best use of prop etc) so that everyone celebrates the other as they would like to be celebrated
- This is a very powerful process in a competitive culture … there are often near tears and true joy as everybody's gifts are held aloft, and all styles of leadership are recognized.

Appendix E   ART EXERCISE

Suggested Time Allotted: 20 mins. + 15 mins. sharing

Materials:
- Large Golden Rule poster
- Handouts of the Golden Rule 8 x 11 sheet (13 religions) for all participants
- 8 x 11 sheets of blank paper
- Magic Markers
- Pencil Crayons
- Crayons
- Rulers

Optional Materials: Magazines for Collage/ Scissors/ Glue sticks / Computer access
Hand out the Golden Rule 8.5 x 11 sheet and display a Golden Rule poster at the front of the room. Make art materials available, as appropriate to students. This exercise can be adapted for use from Grades 1 - 11. Computer graphics & collage art may be employed by more mature students, crayons & colored pencils by junior students.

What would One Global Family - look like?

Some claim that The Golden Rule teaches that Human Beings on the planet, although of different cultures and faiths - are connected to each other in a spirit of unity. The Golden Rule speaks of tolerance, forgiveness, compassion and respect for others. We ask the students to read aloud the Golden Rules in a reflective way, and then to imagine what the world would be like if all peoples recognized that we were connected to each other and to all of creation. What would happen if we all cooperated together as one global family and considered one another brothers and sisters - Global Citizens?

Allow students a minimum of 30 mins for this exercise. At the end of the exercise, have each student participate in a "show and tell." Each student will hold up their artwork or it can be displayed on a Flip - Chart - and explain the meaning of their drawing to the group. In the spirit of the Golden Rule, students are invited to share positive affirmations of what they liked about the particular piece of art.

Pose the question on the chalkboard or flip chart:
What would the world look like if we lived as One Global Family?

NOTES for Retreat Leaders:
Artwork to be on computer paper - 8.5 x 11 in. They can also use poster paper and work as a group. Artwork may include symbols of Golden Rules, text from one or all the faith traditions from the Poster, hand drawn pictures etc. Collage art may include the same.

Additional Suggestions:
Retreat Leaders may choose to hold an art contest and come up with 3 winning place prizes. The Artwork may be laminated and displayed around the room for inspiration or mounted on tri-fold boards for Parents' night. The artwork may be used to create greeting cards to fundraise for school trips or a class booklet .

Appendix F   REFLECTIONS / MEDITATION

Suggested Time Allotted: 5 minute "counting game" to prepare students to be still: a 15 - 20 minute reflection is ideal

Materials:
- a carpeted floor / if no carpet the students are invited to sit with their backs straight on a chair and their feet on the ground.
- dark room, curtains closed
- cd player
- relaxing music - eternal om, chanting, meditative music

Format of Dramatic presentation:
A very integral part to the Golden Rule Retreat is reflection / meditation. Usually teachers marvel at how every single student falls into a deep and radiant relaxed state … even the most fidgety and tightly wound teenager responds to reflection. In fact, those are often the students who benefit most, taking a long time to come out of the blissful state and sharing how it was *"better than sleep"*, *"the most peaceful thing I ever felt"* or *"simply awesome"* … Of course what is awesome is the fact that these young people have allowed themselves to let go enough to have a profound encounter with the light of their own true self … indeed it is the radiance of their own heart that is awesome!

The counting game is a great way to calmly focus the students and instill the great benefits and power or the universal practice of reflection / meditation. Examples of reflections and meditation that work for a Golden Rule Workshop:
- Metta Mediation: extending loving kindness from loved ones - to enemies …
- Tonga Len Meditation: healing yourself and another through intention and breath.
- Body Scan: Grounding Meditation to become aware of the body to relax and *"ground the floating mind."* Just after the Meditation and before the students have fully come out of relaxation, have the students do the counting game once more. The facilitator breaks the silence with saying *"One."* Usually groups surprise themselves by counting much higher after the exercise.

Pose the question on the chalkboard or flip chart:
- How did the counting game prepare you for the meditation?
- Why were we much more successful at the game after the meditation?
- How did you feel entering into the stillness?
- How do you feel now?

NOTES for Retreat Leaders and Additional Suggestions:
Consider a CLOSING CIRCLE before the final song and sending forth. This is a final chance for each member of the community to share one word or phrase about what touched them most about the day. This is a powerful affirmation of themselves, as they get as much out of the day as they put into it … a chance to celebrate each other's gifts and spend a day in the spirit of treating others as you would wish to be treated, and to feel the wonder of being respected by others in the true spirit of the golden rule. The students get a glimpse of how they themselves, and in fact the world, might look if we all truly lived according to the Golden Rule.

Frequently Asked Questions

Who is the target audience of this video?
This video is intended for both adults and students alike. On one level it is meant to provide adults with background information on the Golden Rule as a tool for peace and give them a sense of how this important tool for peace can be engagingly shared with young people. In such a way, it would be of special interest to teachers, youth leaders, chaplains, social workers or anyone working to promote awareness and celebration of cultural diversity.

On another level this video can be used in the classroom with students studying ethics, peace and justice, or world religions. It can also be used prior to attending a Golden Rule Workshop day to prepare the students for the experience and to get them motivated to enter into the day.

Can this video be used for university aged students and if so, how to adapt the exercises?
Yes this video can be used for university students as well as adults. There is something very hopeful in seeing a younger generation eagerly embracing a global consciousness. Since the process we have developed is centered and shaped by the use of symbols, music, poetry, games and movement, the process can be easily adapted to any group - young or old. The process has a universal appeal. With an older group, however, the input section can go deeper and be longer than the recommended 45 minute limit for high school students.

Can this workshop format be adapted to another course I teach?
Yes, this process can be used to explore any topic or issue. You just have to change the input section to match the issue. Then you would shape the other activities to highlight your particular issue. For example, you could end with a song that deals with your issue.

What if I want to include my own exercises?
It is fun coming up with new activities to try out. This keeps the creative juices flowing and the day more interesting to all involved. It is important to make the day your own. This means highlighting your gifts and the activities that interest you. We have discovered that it takes doing a workshop approximately five times before it becomes golden through trial and error.

What if I want to leave out any part of the process?
We have discovered that a successful and satisfying day follows the process we have outlined. Neglecting any of the steps really affects the feel of the day. A couple of times in order to save time we have skipped the use of ice-breaker games that get the students moving and laughing and encourages them to drop some of their self-consciousness. The result was that their skits were not of the same quality as we had previously experienced and they were not able to enter as deeply as usual into the meditative/integrative activity. The day also falls a little flat if you don't send them off with an up beat hopeful song at the end.

Frequently Asked Questions - continued

Can this process be adapted by a teacher/ educator as curriculum for a school term on religion, ethics and justice?

Yes, absolutely! Once you feel comfortable with the basics of this specially designed retreat day, it can be adapted to all sorts of scenarios.

Each classroom period in social justice, values/ ethics or world religions can be dedicated to the exploration of one of the 13 religions on the Golden Rule Poster. For example - a guest speaker who practices or embodies that religion can come in for part of the period, symbols/stories/props can be employed as learning tools, and through 13 - 26 etc classroom periods, each of the 13 religions can be explored in depth, from the perspective of the Golden Rule.

NOTE: we have many excellent downloadable (free) materials geared towards educators on the Scarboro Missions website, located under the area "The Golden Rule." **www.scarboromissions.ca**

Alternately, over several classes, each period can be dedicated to one of the exercises, with the exercises building towards a dramatic presentation at the end of the course or semester. The possibilities are limitless. Once you work your way through the process, it will inspire your own usage of it.

In addition, if the educational institute in question would like to focus its studies on one particular religion, that also can be accommodated by this process.

A guest speaker from one faith tradition can supply the input section (live sharing); props, symbols, costumes and appropriate video materials can be employed, and the exercises contained herein can be adapted to focus on that faith tradition solely.

Animating the Golden Rule across World Religions (Workshop)

In 2013 almost 5,000 young people attended a day workshop at Scarboro Missions. At present we are booked everyday during the school year for Golden Rule Workshops. In order to respond to the increasing demand for these days, it has become clear to us that we need to begin to train more Golden Rule Facilitators. Currently we have trained and involved about a dozen facilitators. We would like to extend our Golden Rule facilitation training to interested youth leaders, ministers, social workers and educators across Canada and internationally.

If you are interested in becoming a Golden Rule facilitator for your own group or community, please contact us to organize audit days or training. If you would like to organize a group that wishes to be trained, it is possible that we may be able to travel to you- upon certain conditions being met.

For Further Info. please contact:
Kathy Murtha - Director
Mission Centre / Scarboro Missions
416.261.7135

Biographies

Mission Centre Director/ Retreat Co-coordinator: KATHY MURTHA

Has worked for over 20 years as a Retreat Director, Workshop Facilitator and Motivational Speaker for young people and adults. Her work has been described as *"inclusive, enriching, engaging and energizing."* She is *"ingenuous at building bridges of peace and understanding."*

Kathy has an MA in history and religious studies from the University of Toronto. As a young adult she spent two years as a volunteer teacher in the Highlands of Papua New Guinea. It was among the Stone Age Huli tribe that she learned the riches and challenges of seeing life through the eyes of *"another."* It was a transformative experience that shaped the course of her life. Upon her return to Canada she initiated a number of self-help groups and workshops for the homeless and marginalized in Toronto, and developed hands-on programs that would bring young people into contact with the human face of poverty and discrimination. For her grass-roots community efforts she received a community award.

The Golden Rule poster, which was created at Scarboro Missions, has become the inspiration and focal point behind the development of a variety of Golden Rule Workshops. A number of creative and enthusiastic artists and presenters have come on board to form a team to respond to the increasing demand for Workshops on the Golden Rule.

Retreat Leader: KATE MARSHALL FLAHERTY

Is an award-winning poet, yoga and meditation instructor, and founding member of the Children's Peace Theatre and retreat facilitator at Scarboro Missions in Toronto. Kate has worked with youth in overseas development work, and with leadership workshops, and brings her skills and gifts to the Golden Rule Workshops at the Golden Rule Institute.

She directed youth for four years as the Art Director of the Mac Drama Guild in Ottawa. She has written curriculum on Conflict Transformation for the Children's Peace Theatre, where she was Programme Director for three years, has four books of poetry published, and has poems in several international anthologies. She also leads "Meditation and Mindfulness" days at University of Toronto Continuing Ed, as well as guides *"Writing as a Spiritual Practice"* series for both adults at Continuing Ed and for the League of Canadian Poets, and with youth as part of the "Poet in the Schools" programme.

She has traveled and worked overseas, taught at the St Lucia School for the Deaf, is a lay member of the Spiritans, and is a life-long student of world religions and the interfaith path.

Guest Speaker / Filmmaker: TINA PETROVA

Has been part of the Canadian Film, TV and Stage scene for over 20 years as an award winning actress, producer, writer and director. She graduated from the Theatre Arts program at Ryerson University, later returning to study Film in the 1990's. She is an Alumni of Norman Jewison's The Canadian Film Centre.

Critics have dubbed Tina a *"driving force"* and *"visionary"*, creating works of *"faith and healing..."*

Her award winning documentary *"RUMI - Turning Ecstatic"* has played in 18 countries to date and been translated into 3 languages, including a special invite to the United Nations in 2007.

"Animating the Golden Rule..." is currently being used as a learning tool in the Canadian High School system and Teachers College training.

Her personal story *"Dancing in the Fire - A Modern Day encounter with RUMI"* is available on KINDLE.

Tina has spoken in auditoriums and on stages around the world and is an impassioned orator. She has personally walked an Interfaith path for the greater part of her adult life- living and working in Native American, Christian, Buddhist, Hindu and Sufi communities.

Her latest book for children "Krista-link-a-la and the Size 13 Shoes" is available in E Book and Paperback. Tina is an accredited Juror for Kids First! Quality Media Coalition. www.tinapetrova.com

Effectiveness of the Program

"The uniqueness of the programme you bring enlivens all who become involved."
- R. Tataski, High School Vice Principal

"I learned so much about peace and respect that I probably would not have known for a very long time... My favorite part was the meditation because it was soooo relaxing. I actually felt like I was in the water and I also felt like I was actually helping to bring peace to the world, or if not to the Whole World at least to the person I was thinking about."
- Alicia S., Student

"I truly enjoyed watching the kids' wheels turning, their minds being bent a little and their having fun and getting closer to each other-all at the same time. Mission accomplished. Congrats on a great program!"
- Maria Louisa H., Teacher and Chaplain

"It was a lot more fun than I expected it to be, and I am really glad I went. At first I thought it would be really boring with a bunch of people talking at us. But I actually learned a lot and really enjoyed it. It made me think of things I never paid much attention to before."
- Jennifer V., Student

"I learned a lot about the Golden Rule and the Underground Railroad. I met people that I hadn't spoken to before and the activities we did were hilarious. I would definitely do it again."
- John T., Student

"My class thoroughly enjoyed the experience as did I. What I found to be valuable and inspirational was the embodiment of the Golden Rule by my students. Their interpretation of the different religious exclamations of the Golden Rule was inspirational. Through mime, dance, song, movement and the spoken word the Golden Rule of Baha'i, Jainism and Native Spirituality became alive ... a lived experience. It allowed my students to work together, to collaborate and to learn in a friendly and safe environment."
- Marylyn G., Teacher and Chaplain

"Thank you for letting me experience a spiritual emotional side of me that I don't tend to reveal. It was inspirational."
- Shauna K., Student

"It was cool how people dressed up."
- Michael S., Student

"The retreat was a very inspiring experience because it showed me things I was blind to before ... During the retreat learned how to get in touch with my deeper self and build a whole new perspective on life and what the media feeds our minds."
- Kenneth G., Student

"My favorite part of the whole retreat was the meditation, because once I got into it - all my stress left my body. I have never been to something like that and I didn't think that it would work, but it did, and I thank you for that."
- Jonathon, Student

"Thank you for a very, very good time yesterday. I had a blast! Projects, ISUS and school itself started getting to me to the point where I would just snap. You helped me get away from the stress and be free from all other thoughts. The games we played were very unique and very fun. Yesterday, I became much closer to my classmates and fellow students, and I would just like to thank you for that."
- Jennifer S., Student

Some Resources

"A Song of Peace" – Zehnder Music DVD.   www.ztheband.com

"Playing for Change" - CD/DVD - all songs were recorded live by musicians from around the world. We especially like to use *"One Love"* as a send off song. We get the students to dance or play along with instruments that we supply (drums, tambourines, shakers)   www.playingforchange.com

Picture of the Earth from Space. - Still photos. One Earth with no boundaries. You can get beautiful images of the earth from space on the Internet. They can be incorporated into a power point and projected on a screen as a focal point and reminder throughout the day.

Pachabel's Canon - Music CD (Ocean sounds).

Music CDs by Robert Gass

"Deepening Stillness" a CD of Guided Meditation and Poetry by Katie Marshall Flaherty.
Big Window Music, composed by Mark Korven   www.scarboromissions.ca

Tina Petrova's DVD *"Rumi: Turning Ecstatic"*   www.rumi-turningecstatic.com

Ryan Nutter's *"Golden Rule Interactive Flash"* - with accompanying music from each faith tradition
www. scarboro missions.ca

"Releasing the Captives: Taking Action on Trafficking of Women and Children," Making Waves, vol 6:2.   www.wicc.org

"Being a Global Village: Human Trafficking and the 2010 Olympics," – an interactive awareness and action kit for high school students produced by the Canadian Religious Conference in conjunction with the School Sisters of Notre Dame. Go to website www.crc-canada.org, click on Priorities and then click on **Trafficking** to order.

"Shiva Nataraj: Lord of the Dance & OM: Sound of the Sacred," - CD produced by Encounter World Religion Centre in Guelph, Ontario.   www.worldreligons.ca

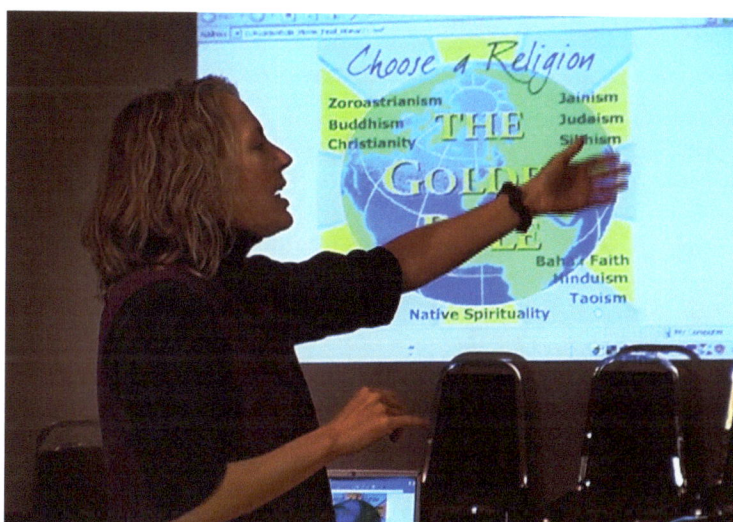

For further information on Golden Rule Retreat days for Youth & Golden Rule Facilitator training please contact:

Mission Centre
Scarboro Missions
2685 Kingston Road
Toronto, ON
M1M 1M4
Canada

416.261.7135

Guidebook Authors

Kathy Murtha
Katie Marshall Flaherty
Tina Petrova

The DVD
Animating the Golden Rule.....An Introduction

is available both as a single DVD with useful extra materials for the classroom as well as a DVD/ Teachers Guidebook Package, to assist educators using the video in class

Please visit: **www.thegoldenrulemovie.com** for further information on the DVD materials.

French subtitled version available.
English Version with subtitles for the hard of hearing.

Teacher's Notes

Teacher's Notes

Follow Our Journey !

f Facebook: Golden Rule Poster

🐦 Twitter: @goldenrulemovie

www.thegoldenrulemovie.com